STOP.
AF604607
YAY!

HUH?

ASKS THE QUESTION MARK

BY ROB LISLE

First Published 2026 by
Redback Publishing
Suite 6, 13a Narabang Way,
Belrose NSW 2085
Australia

www.redbackpublishing.com
orders@redbackpublishing.com

ISBN 978-1-761402-12-8

Author: Rob Lisle
Editor: Simone Saba
Designer: Redback Publishing
Illustrator: Rob Lisle

Originated by Redback Publishing

A catalogue record for this book is available from the National Library of Australia

HUH?
ASKS THE QUESTION MARK

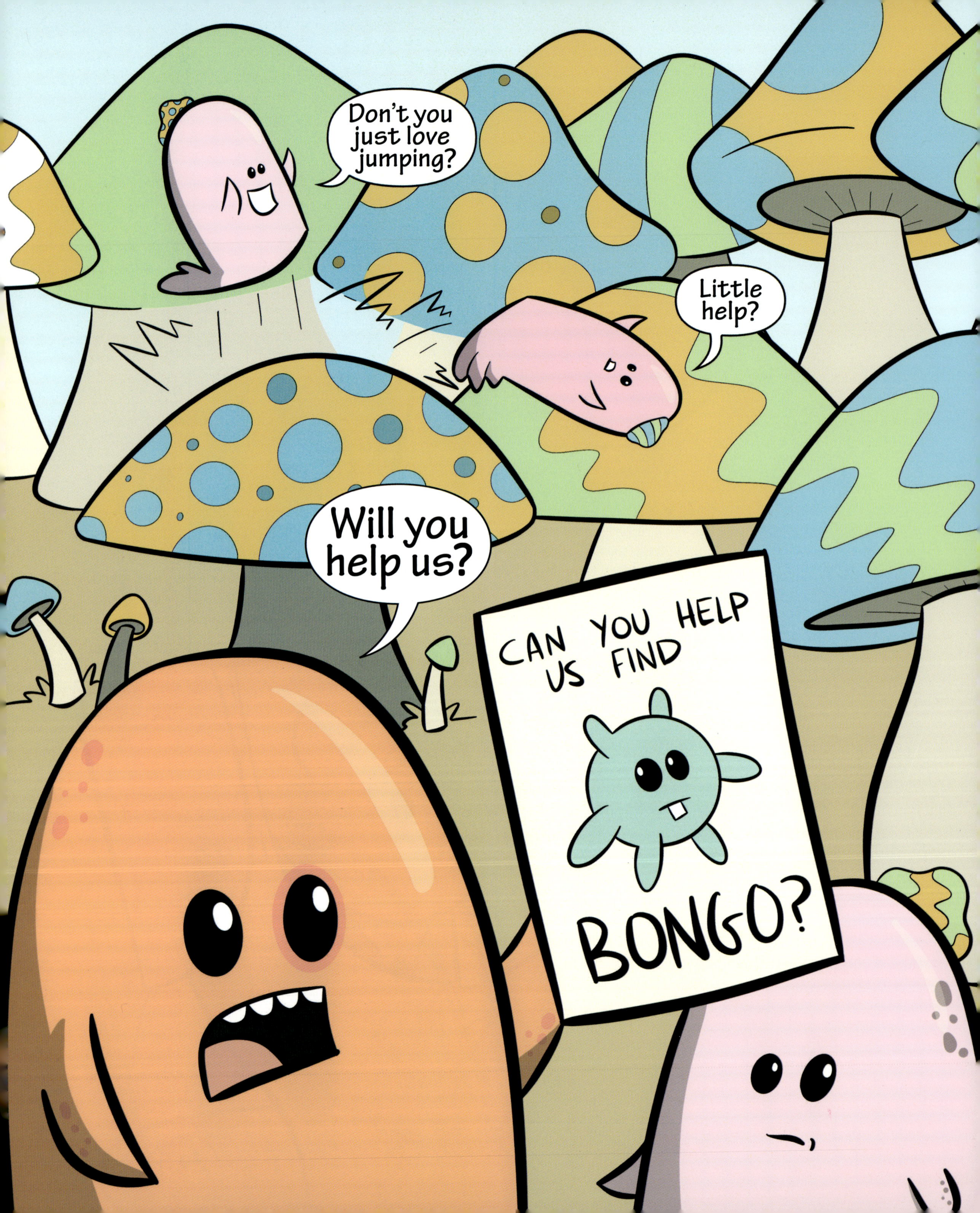
Don't you just love jumping?
Little help?
Will you help us?
CAN YOU HELP US FIND
BONGO?

We all have questions. And what do all questions have in common? **The question mark.**
Do you like mushrooms?
Hello?
Have you seen my pet, Bongo?
What is that?
Should we head out on a quest to find Bongo?

Sometimes a question is short and added to the end of a sentence.

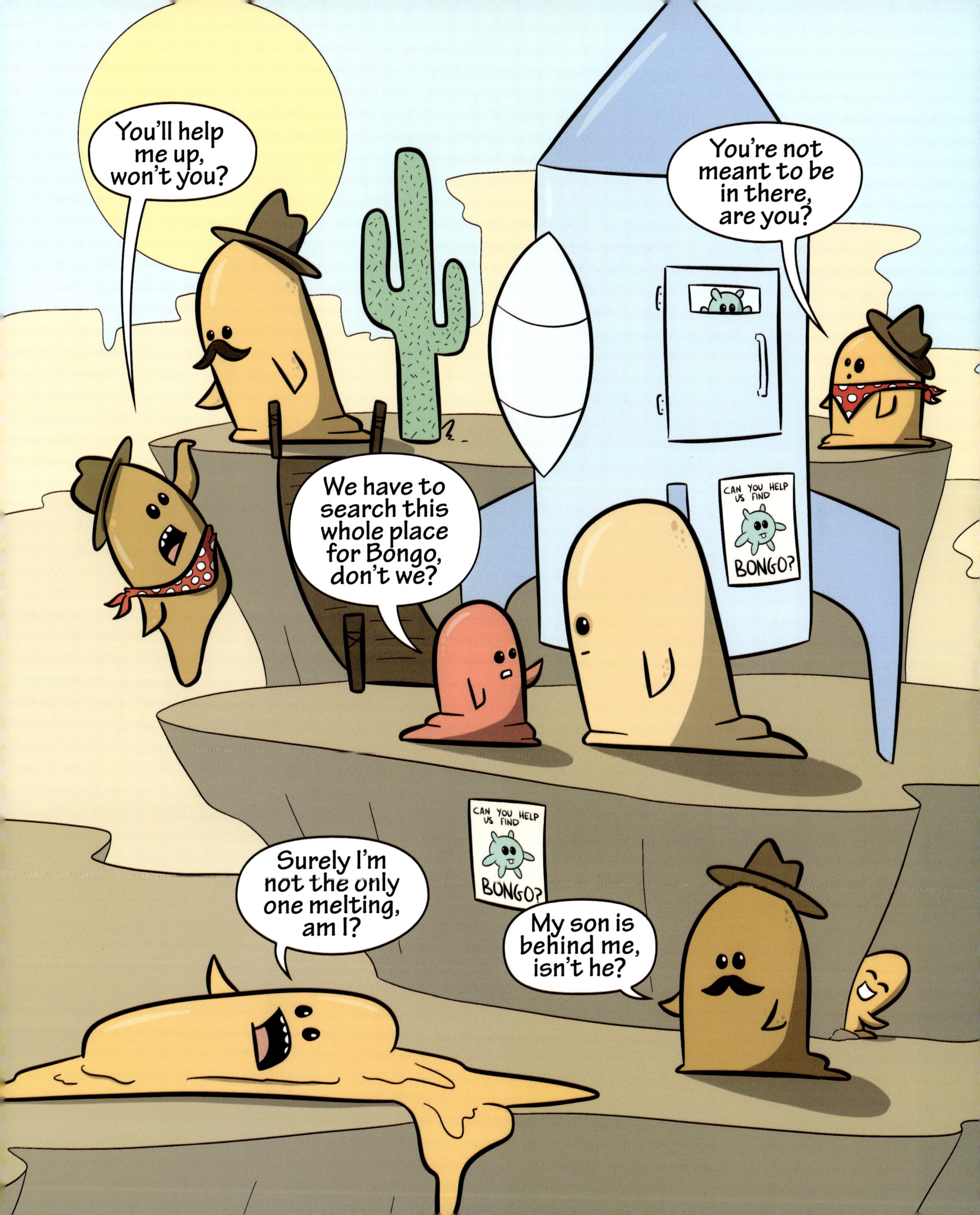
You'll help me up, won't you?
You're not meant to be in there, are you?
We have to search this whole place for Bongo, don't we?
CAN YOU HELP US FIND BONGO?
CAN YOU HELP US FIND BONGO?
Surely I'm not the only one melting, am I?
My son is behind me, isn't he?

Some questions can be answered with a simple **YES** or **NO**.

Is it hammer time yet?
No.
Are you okay to keep going?
Yes.
Have you got it?
Yes.
GYM
Would you like to join the gym?
No.
MEMBERSHIPS $7,000
Am I the coolest dude ever?
No.

Question marks are used when we are asking about a time.

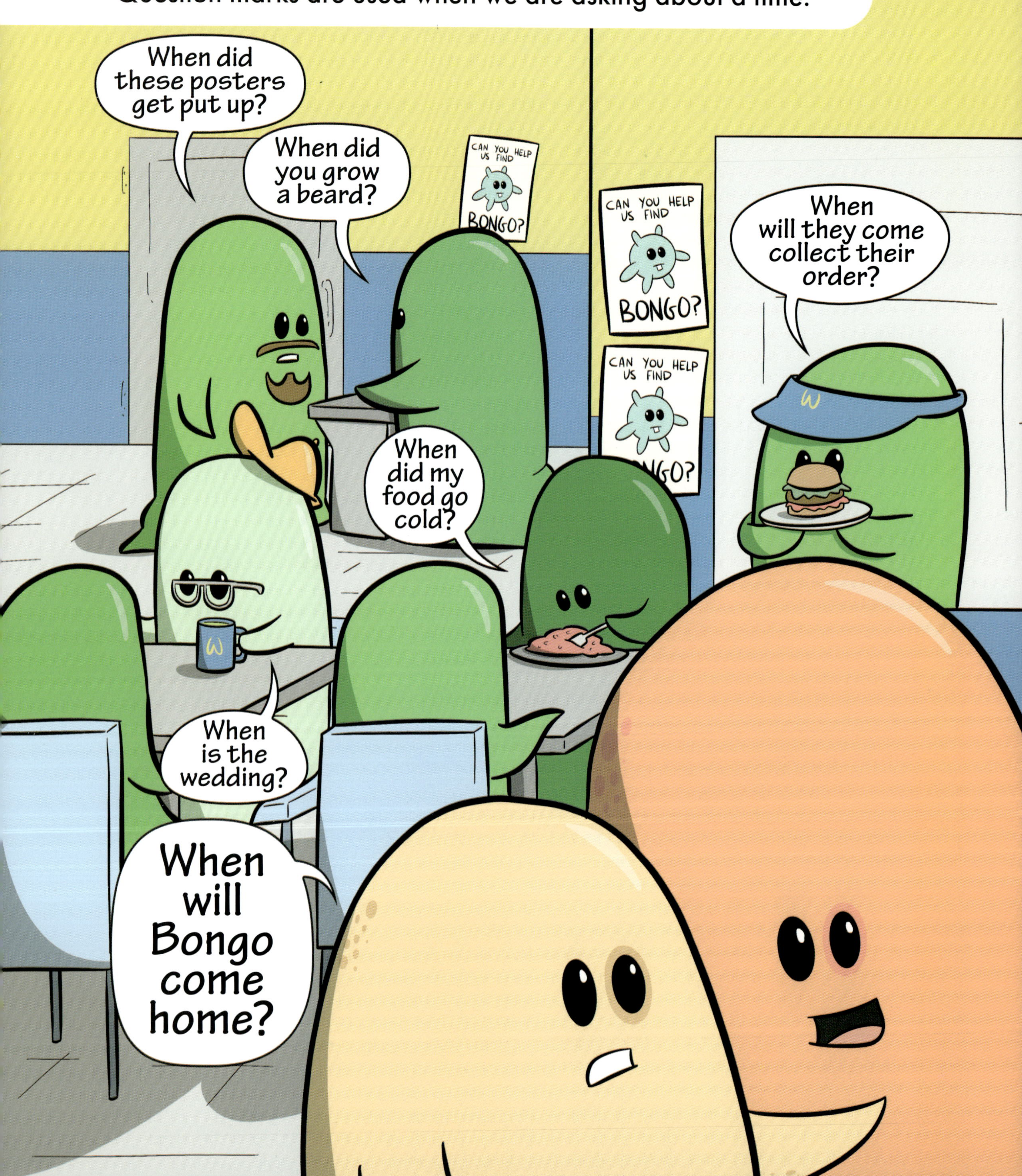

CAN YOU HELP US FIND BONGO?
CAN YOU HELP US FIND BONGO?
CAN YOU HELP US FIND BONGO?
When would you like the burger?
PLEASE WASH YOUR FEET
When will the fries be ready?
When do you need it by?
When do you close?
When did we last have burgers?
When will you get off the phone?
When will we find Bongo?

Question marks are used when we are asking about a place.

Where are we headed next?
Where did you come from?
Where did my spanner go?
Where am I?
Where have I tasted this before?

Question marks are used when we are asking about a reason or cause.

Why do monkeys like bananas so much?
Why don't you eat something?
Why am I so hungry?
Why do I have to be scared of heights?
Why are you doing that?
CAN YOU HELP US FIND BONGO?
CAN YOU HELP US FIND BONGO?
Why is the sky blue?
DO NOT USE A FULL STOP (.) WITH A QUESTION MARK.
WHY IS THE SKY BLUE?.
WHY IS THE SKY BLUE?
Why do we have to go to school today?
Why?

Question marks are used when asking how something is done, how much of something there is, or what kind or condition it's in.

How do you know which way to go?
How does a chicken breathe under water?
Bok?
How do I carry all of this?
How are you?

Question marks are used when we are asking about a person or an animal.
Who?
Who?
Who?
Who lives in that scary house?
CAN YOU HELP US FIND BONGO?
Who's a good kitty?

Who here has seen our pet, Bongo?
Who?
Who let the owls out?
Who?
Who?
Who?
Who?
Who left these pumpkins here?
DO NOT USE A QUESTION MARK IN STATEMENTS.
I WONDER WHO SAW BONGO LAST?
I WONDER WHO SAW BONGO LAST.

Questions can help us find out more about friends and family.

How arrrgh ye?
Squawk?
What are you squawking about?
How did you get up there?
Are you ok?
Did you want to get dinner after this?
What would you like to eat?
How are the kids?
Good. And yours?

A **rhetorical question** is asked in order to create a dramatic effect or to make a point rather than to get an answer.

Isn't this a fine mess?
Can you imagine a life without Bongo and his friends?
THEY SAID
"WHO CARES?"
When quoting a question, the question mark goes inside the quotation marks.
Who's a good boy?
Who doesn't like a story with a happy ending?

Learning starts with a question.

Should we turn the page?

Now that you're a QUESTION MARK master, can you use your new skills to give these characters a voice?

Flip back through the book to find these scenes.

ACTIVITIES

TURN IT INTO A QUESTION!

OBJECTIVE	Learn how to turn a statement into a question.
STEPS	• Provide a list of statements. • Ask children to think about what question could be asked about each statement. • Children rewrite each statement as a question beginning with a question word or helping verb (Do, Can, Is, etc.).
BONUS ACTIVITY	Students can choose a fact they know and turn it into a pop quiz for their friends to answer.

EXAMPLE

Statement:
Bongo is lost.

Question:
Is Bongo lost?

COMMAND OR QUESTION?

OBJECTIVE	Know the difference between a command (telling) and a question (asking).
STEPS	• Tell the kids to select five questions from the book and write them out on a piece of paper. • Kids are then to turn the question into a command. • Remind them to use the correct punctuation!
BONUS ACTIVITY	Encourage children to keep a 'Question or Command' tally chart for things you hear throughout the day.

EXAMPLES

Question:
Have you seen Bongo?

Command:
Tell me if you've seen Bongo

Question:
You'll help me up, won't you?

Command:
Help me up.

ASK THE OBJECT!

OBJECTIVE	Write your own questions using question marks.

STEPS

- Tell children to choose a character from any scene in the book. It could be a main character or someone in the background.
- Tell them to think of three things they'd like to ask that character.
- Ask them to write their questions, starting with question words and using question marks.

EXAMPLE

Character:
Astronaut

Questions:
What's your favourite planet?
How did you get here?
Why are those cords attached to you?

BONUS ACTIVITY

Children can draw the object or animal and write their questions in a speech bubble next to it.

QUESTION STARTERS

OBJECTIVE	Identify and use question words like Who, What, Where, When, Why and How.

STEPS

- Ask children to identify as many question words as they can (e.g. Who, What, Where).
- Tell them to use each word at the beginning of a sentence and write down a question.
- Remind them to end the sentence with a question mark.

EXAMPLE

Word:
Where

Your question:
Where did Bongo go?

BONUS ACTIVITY

In groups or pairs, children can make a colourful 'Question Words' poster. They should include one sentence for each of the question words.

NARRATIVE TEXT

Deep in the ocean the search for Bongo continued, and what did our determined searchers see there?

They saw a big octopus, some ocean explorers and a wrecked ship that looked like it once belonged to Vikings. Aren't these strange findings?

Bongo's owners immediately set out looking for their pet. They looked high and low, in caves and in the wreckage. They passed out pamphlets, hoping someone had seen Bongo.

The ocean dwellers, however, were too busy thinking of other things to help them.

"How do I know the treasure isn't in here if I don't check?" asked one of the divers as he swam into a cave.

With no help from the others, they looked and looked, but still, they could not find Bongo.

How terrible is that?

"How are we going to find Bongo?" sighed Bongo's owner.

"How are we talking under water?" wondered their friend.

REAL OR RHETORICAL?

OBJECTIVE	Understand the difference between genuine questions and rhetorical ones.
STEPS	• Have the kids read the provided narrative based on a spread from the book. • Have them underline all question words and question marks and determine whether it is a real or rhetoric question. • Is someone expecting an answer? • Or is it a rhetorical question meant to make a point or express something?
BONUS ACTIVITY	Students pair up and each create a list with a mix of real or rhetorical questions. They read them aloud and their partner must determine what kind of question it is.

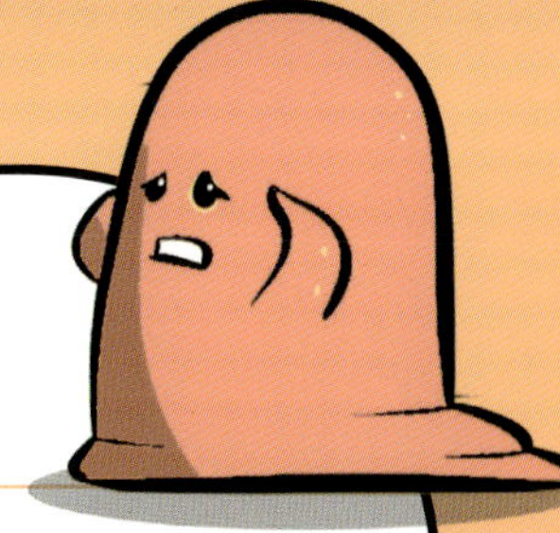

QUESTION MATCH GAME

OBJECTIVE	Match answers to possible questions to understand sentence structure.	
STEPS	• Ask children to write 5 answers on slips of paper (e.g. 'In the treasure chest', 'A monkey', 'Bongo'). • Have them mix up the slips of paper and lay them out for their friend. • Children are to select one another's pieces of paper and try to find a question from the book that could match it.	**EXAMPLE** Answer: In the treasure chest. Question: Do you know where Bongo is?
BONUS ACTIVITY	Turn it into a group activity – one person writes the answers and the others race to write the matching questions!	

THE FIVE W'S AND ONE H

OBJECTIVE	Learn that most questions start with Who, What, When, Where, Why or How.	
STEPS	• Have kids flip through the book and search for questions that do not begin with Who, What, When, Where, Why or How. • Tell the kids to write these questions down. • They should then rewrite the questions using Who, What, When, Where, Why or How.	**EXAMPLE** Found: You don't have to shout, do you? Your question: Why are you shouting?
BONUS ACTIVITY	Children may now do the opposite! Tell them to go back through the book and find questions that begin with Who, What, When, Where, Why or How, and rewrite them using different words.	

Is there more?
COLLECT ALL THE BOOKS IN THE PUNCTUATION EXPEDITION SERIES!
PUNCTUATION EXPEDITION
HUH?
ASKS THE QUESTION MARK
How?
Who?
Where?
What?
Why?
ROB LISLE
PUNCTUATION EXPEDITION
STOP.
COMMANDS THE FULL STOP
Stop.
Woof.
Halt.
ROB LISLE
PUNCTUATION EXPEDITION
WAIT,
SAYS THE COMMA
Wait,
Breathe,
Pause,
ROB LISLE
PUNCTUATION EXPEDITION
YAY!
SHOUTS THE EXCLAMATION MARK
Yay!
Wow!
Woo!
Yeah!
Oink!
ROB LISLE

WAIT,
HUH?